SPECIAL EDUCATIONAL NEEDS

POLICY OPTIONS STEERING GROUP

POLICY PAPER 2
(third series)

Developments in Additional Resource Allocation to Promote Greater Inclusion

A NASEN PUBLICATION

Published in 2000

ISBN 1 901485 15 3

Published by NASEN.
NASEN is a company limited by guarantee, registered in England and Wales. Company No. 2674379.
NASEN is a registered charity. Charity No. 1007023.

Further copies of this book and details of NASEN's many other publications may be obtained from the Publications Department at its registered office: NASEN House, 4/5, Amber Business Village, Amber Close, Amington, Tamworth, Staffs. B77 4RP.
Tel: 01827 311500; Fax: 01827 313005
Email: welcome@nasen.org.uk
Web site: www.nasen.org.uk

Cover design by Graphic Images.
Typeset in Times by J. C. Typesetting and printed in the United Kingdom by Stowes.

Special Educational Needs Policy Options Steering Group

Developments in Additional Resource Allocation to Promote Greater Inclusion

POLICY PAPER 2
(third series)

Edited by Brahm Norwich

Contents

Chapter 1
Introduction to Policy Paper

This paper is a record of the recent invited Policy Seminar held at the Institute of Education, London University (20th July 1999) which examined the question of Developments in Resource Allocation. It was the second seminar in the third round of these SEN Policy Option Seminar series. The aim of the seminar was to reconsider this fundamental issue in the light of new developments since we last considered resource allocation as a topic in the first series (by Ingrid Lunt and Jennifer Evans, see first series details below). The Steering Group decided to focus on resource allocation following the publication of the SEN Action Plan and the Government's commitment to inclusion and in the context of the changes in school funding.

The main paper was presented by John Moore, who is well known for his work in Kent on resource allocation systems. We had three discussants from different perspectives. We invited Dr Cor Meijer from Holland, who is known for his European work, Professor Paul Croll and Dr Diana Moses, who have conducted research relating to this topic, and Professor Klaus Wedell who has had a long-standing interest in such questions. In addition to the main paper and three discussants' papers, there is a brief summary of the general discussion.

About 50 people participated in the day seminar, coming from schools, LEA support services, LEA officers, DfEE, Government Agencies, parent groups, the voluntary sector, health service professionals, educational psychologists and universities.

SEN Policy Options Steering Group
Background

This policy paper is the second in the third series of seminars and conferences to be organised by the SEN Policy Options Steering Group. This group organised the initial ESRC-Cadbury Trust series on policy options for special educational needs in the 1990s. The success of the first series led to the second one which was supported financially by NASEN. (See the list of these policy papers published by NASEN at the end of this section.) The Steering Group has representatives from LEA administrators, head teachers, voluntary organisations, professional associations, universities and research. The further success of the second series of policy seminars and papers led to this round of seminars which has also been organised with further funding from NASEN. These events are intended to consider current and future policy issues in the field in a proactive way. They are planned to interest all those concerned with policy matters in special educational needs.

Aims and objectives of the Policy Options Group

1. to identify current and likely future policy problems and the options for solutions in special education provision following the Green Paper 1997 through to the year 2000 and beyond;

2. to organise conferences and seminars for policy-makers, professionals, parents, voluntary associations and researchers in the field and publish the proceedings for wider dissemination;

3. to enhance the two-way relationship between policy and service issues and research agendas.

Current Steering Group membership
Mr Keith Bovair, Head teacher Durrants School (NASEN representative); Mr Clive Danks, Advisor, Birmingham LEA; Mr Tony Dessent, Director of Education, Luton LEA; Dr Seamus Hegarty, Director of the National Foundation for Educational Research; Professor Geoff Lindsay, Warwick University; Dr Ingrid Lunt, Reader, Institute of Education, London University; Mr Vincent McDonnell, Director of Education, Richmond LEA; Mr Chris Marshall (OFSTED); Professor Brahm Norwich, School of Education, Exeter University; Mrs Margaret Peter; Mrs Philippa Russell, Director of Council for Disabled Children; Professor Klaus Wedell, Institute of Education, London University.

Current series
The current series aims to organise four full or half-day events on special education policy and provision over the two years 1998/99 - 1999/2000 which are relevant to the context of considerable changes in the education system.
If you have any ideas about possible topics or would like to know more about the events, please do contact a member of the Group or Brahm Norwich at the School of Education, University of Exeter, Heavitree Road, Exeter EX1 2LU (email b.norwich@exeter.ac.uk).

Policy Options Papers from first seminar series published and available from NASEN

1. **Bucking the Market: LEAs and Special Needs**
   Peter Housden, Chief Education Officer, Nottinghamshire LEA.

2. **Towards Effective Schools for All**
   Mel Ainscow, Cambridge University Institute of Education.

3. **Teacher Education for Special Educational Needs**
   Professor Peter Mittler, Manchester University.

4. **Allocating Resources for SEN Provision**
   Jennifer Evans and Ingrid Lunt, Institute of Education, London University.

5. **Planning and Diversity: Special Schools and Their Alternatives**
   Max Hunt, Director of Education, Stockport LEA.

6. **Options for Partnership between Health, Education and Social Services**
   Tony Dessent, Senior Assistant Director, Nottinghamshire LEA.

7. **Provision for Special Educational Needs from the Perspectives of Service Users**
   Micheline Mason, Robina Mallet, Colin Low and Philippa Russell.

Policy Options Papers from second seminar series published and available from NASEN

1. **Independence and Interdependence? Responsibilities for SEN in the Unitary and County Authorities**
   Roy Atkinson, Michael Peters, Derek Jones, Simon Gardner and Philippa Russell.

2. **Inclusion or Exclusion: Future Policy for Emotional and Behavioural Difficulties**
   John Bangs, Peter Gray and Greg Richardson.

3. **Baseline Assessment: Benefits and Pitfalls**
   Geoff Lindsay, Max Hunt, Sheila Wolfendale, Peter Tymms.

4. Future Policy for SEN: Responding to the Green Paper
Brahm Norwich, Ann Lewis, John Moore, Harry Daniels.

Policy Options Papers from third seminar series published and available from NASEN

1. Rethinking Support for More Inclusive Schooling
Peter Gray, Clive Danks, Rik Boxer, Barbara Burke, Jeff Frank, Ruth Newbury, Joan Baxter.

Chapter 2
Developments in Additional Resource Allocation to Promote Greater Inclusion

JOHN MOORE, Senior Inspector, Kent LEA

Introduction

In the first series of seminars, Jennifer Evans and Ingrid Lunt (Evans & Lunt, 1994) provided a well-researched and comprehensive overview of the issues surrounding the funding of SEN. They traced events from the publication of the *Warnock Report* to the *Education Act 1993*, exploring the issues of *which* pupils to resource and *how* to allocate these resources from a finite budget. Usefully they concluded with a list of 11 principles. These are still relevant and are:

- transparency and clarity;

- rational and coherent planning across mainstream and special schools;

- minimal identification of pupils;

- protecting resourcing for the small minority with severe and complex needs;

- resourcing a wider group through differential resourcing of schools;

- clarifying the respective responsibilities of LEA and schools;

- monitoring and evaluation of devolved management;

- monitoring and evaluation of cost and success of different forms of provision;

- economies of scale;

- equality of opportunity;

- equity of allocation.

Clive Danks also argued that 'SEN is not synonymous with need' and that inclusion demands that resources be allocated to the whole pupil cohort. In addition, Philippa Russell, in her summary of the discussion, made clear the connection between the move towards a locally based, community approach to meeting needs and the inevitability of inter-agency funding. Both these viewpoints are important because they are consistent with the broader view of Social Inclusion promoted by the current Government, which itself may affect our view of funding.

Much has happened, of course, since that seminar. We now have:

- statutory target setting with a national strategy for the teaching of literacy, numeracy and ICT and more sophisticated comparative data used by schools to judge value added;

- multi-agency initiatives such as Children's Services, Early Years Development and Child Care Plans, Quality Protects and new policies and initiatives for Social Services and Health;

- Education Action Zones, New Start and increased access to pre-school;

- OFSTED inspection of the LEA and significant changes to the OFSTED inspection of schools;

- an agenda for the future of special schools, revision of the *Code of Practice* and the furthering of inclusion through a partnership approach;

- more joined-up thinking in relation to social exclusion and national strategies for social inclusion and family support;

- Education Development Plans for LEAs, requirements on LEAs to produce a policy on inclusion and a Support Plan, and a new set of roles for LEAs defined by Government in relation to school improvement;

- a national Programme of Action for SEN and radical proposals for post-16 organisation and funding.

Common threads are 'required' plans, underpinned by ambitious targets, accompanied by funding, often via a bid, from central Government. Most of these initiatives also require multi-agency involvement. Before exploring the impact of these further, however, I want to return to some of the milestones dealt with by Lunt and Evans and comment on them from a local authority perspective. These concern the strategic link between local authority objectives for SEN and funding.

Local authorities and funding objectives

Methods of funding additional needs have changed over the last 18 years, and I would suggest in three stages. Initially, following the *Warnock Report* and the *Education Act 1981*, there was a need to look more closely at how mainstream schools were identifying and providing for the 18% of children described by the Warnock Report as having special educational needs. It is easy to forget that many mainstream schools did not have ways of identifying and supporting these children and that as a result many children were excluded from otherwise worthwhile activities. An early consideration, therefore, was to improve the ability of mainstream schools to identify and provide for these pupils. In Kent, a great deal of thought was given to how this might be done and also to the issue of underfunding. A mechanism had to be found which would, over time, increase the amount of money allocated to mainstream schools and encourage a more positive response to identified need. An objective was set and the SEN Audit was developed. Local management did not exist; neither did the National Curriculum. At that time it seemed legitimate to promote the culture of 'financial incentive'. This strategy very quickly enhanced schools' capability and a real growth in budget took place despite increased pressure on public finances.

The second phase came about through the need to promote integration. Once schools were used to identifying need and developing systems to meet these, it was a natural progression to retain more children within the mainstream setting. As a result the budget began to grow at a very significant rate as schools were provided with substantial resources, often in the form of learning support assistants. In Kent, the SEN Audit played its part by extending the incentive model into statutory assessment, but it was necessary to supplement this system with more sophisticated funding related to bands of need.

These approaches to funding, however, required more complex methods of decision-making and soon we were into the formal structures that now epitomise the 'bureaucracy' associated with the five stages of the *Code of Practice.*

The third phase was linked to school improvement and the need to demonstrate outcomes, which coincidentally had grown alongside the argument for inclusion. This had begun well before the Government had

11

produced its Green Paper, *Excellence for All* (DfEE, 1997). The objective here was to promote achievement for all and move the current system away from integration towards inclusion. As a result, it became clear that decision-making procedures and the working patterns of schools and support services had to change, and that the key to this change was funding.

It could be argued, therefore, that given the circumstances, a period of perverse incentives was necessary. This is reinforced by Crowther, Dyson and Millward (1998) in their recent DfEE report on funding pupils with MLD. They point out that Warnock promoted a direct linkage between an assessment of a child's learning difficulties and the provision that these demand.

'Indeed, the concept of "special educational need" is itself the embodiment of this linkage, since the "need" in question arises out of the child's difficulties, and is a need for provision of a particular kind.'

Warnock never envisaged the need for clearly defined educational outcomes. Today's agenda, however, is very much about outcomes and that will, by necessity, alter our approach to the systems employed, and to the monitoring of resource-allocation and resource-usage.

What can we learn from this? First, that the funding mechanism has to fit the desired objective for change rather than the most obvious cost-effective route to meeting individual pupil needs. Second, that the successive changes in funding strategy were probably necessary in the light of how schools develop and that a more direct route to inclusion may not have worked. Third, that funding inclusion as part of school improvement is very different to funding integration and that a local authority must have a clear understanding of the difference if it is to succeed in moving inclusion forward.

This is a view endorsed by the recent DfEE-sponsored study (Ainscow, Farrell, Tweddle & Malki, 1999) into LEA policies on inclusion. What should be of concern, however, is the finding of that report that 'local authorities remain confused about what is meant by inclusion in relation to education provision.' I would venture to suggest that there is little in the Government's *Programme of Action*, beyond the more general view of a 'local inclusive network', to guide them, and that we are likely to see as many interpretations and responses to inclusion as there are ways of describing special educational needs.

We have a position, then, where the funding mechanisms chosen by a local authority will determine the outcomes of its response to inclusion, but where, as yet, there is insufficient clarity of objectives to inform that mechanism. The Government requirement for Education Development

Plans and specifically, an Inclusion Support Plan, will aid the process but it will not necessarily bring an authority to the point where the consequences of any particular interpretation of inclusion are made apparent to parents, pupils, schools and services. Whether inclusion means neighbourhood; changing teachers' behaviour, attitudes and skills; working on peer acceptance of individual difference; cluster working; greater responsibility at the local level; or something entirely different, it will ultimately shape funding.

Deciding on need

Notwithstanding the above, resources cannot be allocated equitably, effectively and efficiently until the differential needs of schools have been identified. In the light of the Government's decision not to introduce national descriptors for SEN, local authorities are left to make far-reaching decisions about the nature of SEN. That this is no easy task is evidenced in the recent difficulties encountered by the Teacher Training Agency in their attempts to introduce national standards for 'specialist SEN' training. If professionals in the field cannot agree on how special educational needs should be described for the purposes of training, what level of sophistication can we expect of officers and members of a local authority who must do this before attempting to devise funding mechanisms?

Further, it is not helpful that the current debate on inclusion should fall into two camps. A local authority cannot develop funding mechanisms that solely relate to contextual factors surrounding mainstream education, no more than it can continue with systems that allocate resources solely on the basis of categories of need. On a day-to-day basis, it is self-evident to most teachers that their approach to teaching and learning must take into account some 'within child' factors. It is not reasonable to expect them to view inclusion entirely from the perspective of their own approach to the organisation of teaching and learning. I would agree, therefore, with Brahm Norwich's (Norwich, 1999) recent comment made whilst reviewing two new books on inclusion, that he:

'would welcome debates within special education which go beyond these continuing dichotomies, so we start to grapple with when it is better to think in terms of situated difficulties in learning and when in terms of pervasive learning difficulties'.

Local authorities will also need to reconsider the criteria for resource allocation in the light of Fair Funding, and the more recent pressure brought about by the publication of LEA league tables on spending and delegation patterns. Most would also see a need to improve the balance between the proportions of funding to be withheld for Statements of SEN and the basic amount allocated to schools for the purposes of educating all children. Given an environment of more restricted budgets, this balance is crucial to achieving inclusion objectives. Too much delegated to schools will leave the local authority vulnerable to overspend on statutory assessment mid-year, particularly in the light of more stringent audit commission completion indicators. Too little will fuel the expectations of schools and parents that inclusion will be underwritten by the local authority through statutory assessment, a position which many local authorities find counter-productive to developing an inclusive culture in schools. Get the balance wrong and inclusion becomes an effort for schools, which stops at the limits of local authority support.

A definition of need that might better meet the aims of inclusion, therefore, would be one that moves away from the traditional descriptors associated with special educational need. First, it would place less emphasis on the individual child and be more institutionally based. Financial support and service support would address itself to the whole school, or the whole community of schools within a locality. Second, it would promote school effectiveness strategies and focus on teaching and learning for diversity. Third, it would enable resources to be deployed effectively without recourse to statutory assessment. Fourth, it would avoid, as much as possible, registering children as having special educational needs, so that they are not singled out as educational failures. Fifth, it would provide a more secure basis for increased levels of joint funding.

To achieve this we may have to move away from describing needs as 'special', perhaps developing a broader definition of 'educational need' - one that replaces the current sharp distinction between SEN and other aspects of need such as disaffection, social exclusion, looked after children, traveller education, school exclusion and English as an additional language.

Redefining support

How support is perceived and used by schools is also critical to the success of inclusion. A number of recent studies have questioned the efficacy of 1:1 pupil support by a special support assistant. Apart from the question of learned dependence there is the substantial issue of removed responsibility, since such support is not always effective in encouraging the teacher to include the child within the full range of learning activities. Where local authorities have not delegated funds for Statemented pupils in the ways suggested by Evans and Lunt, for example, they have been drawn, largely by the school's view of 'additional' and 'different', to providing support through a learning support assistant.

There are at least two issues here. The first pertains to the appropriateness of such an approach in meeting identified needs; the second raises questions about the management of resources and the efficiency of attaching a resource to an individual child. As regards the first, on the one hand, it is difficult to see how an individual assistant can promote inclusion unless s/he is supporting the inclusion of all pupils in the classroom by supporting the teacher in their planning and delivery of the curriculum. On the other, it is clear that some pupils with exceptional levels of need, such as those related to social communication disorders, will not be brought into a situation of genuine peer group learning unless there is some specific intervention to aid this. Although Norwich's comments are aimed at those who theorise and therefore conceptualise special education, his observations are equally relevant to the classroom. In questioning the relationship between organic physical functioning and learning in a social context, he is also asking how a child with very significantly different ways of functioning can be supported. For the most part, this balance between individual pupil support and support to the environment to enable inclusion has not been achieved. Changes to funding must address this.

The second issue, that of the poor management of non-delegated resources deployed to meet needs identified in a Statement of SEN, is not one that can be entirely blamed on local authorities. As indicated earlier, funding mechanisms have developed to meet the changing expectations of successive governments. The future of statutory assessment, sometimes referred to as the 'central motivator', remains entirely outside of the control of local authorities, who will continue to struggle if it continues in its present form. Whatever mechanisms a local authority may devise to ensure an appreciation of finite budgets and provide equity of distribution, it is likely to be challenged at some point in relation to an individual child. Nevertheless, a clear message needs to be given to schools and parents that it is impossible for any local authority to maintain long-term and continued SEN growth without there being a significant effect on mainstream school budgets or other important areas of Council spending.

Delegation and support services

Despite these difficulties, local authorities will need to give more attention to methods of delegation that place the sum of the resource available for Statement support in the hands of a school or group of schools. To do this it will have to issue clearer guidance on what is expected within the context of local authority policy on inclusion and more attention will need to be given to what constitutes 'quality' in intervention. Schools need to establish a way of assessing whether progress is acceptable relative to the starting point. Perhaps some pupils have a right to be slower in their progress than others, and that is an acceptable part of difference. Such a view, and I am not proposing a return to a culture of low expectations, might help a school or group of schools to better determine priorities within a finite budget. The job of the local authority would then be one of ensuring that Statements of SEN reflect contextual factors, for example, the amount of support already available in a particular school and any economies of scale that could be achieved by pupils sharing resources.

As part of its policy statement on SEN funding, NASEN (1998) promotes positive discrimination in favour of pupils with SEN. To quote, 'to enable them to learn, children with special educational needs require more resources than their peers'. In the light of the foregoing, however, we need to question the concept of special educational needs as a separate funding mechanism. If schools are to be encouraged to manage their resources more flexibly and services are to be encouraged to work more closely together to enable schools to provide a more inclusive environment, then a more holistic method of funding is also required. Whether it is possible to assess the needs of a group of schools so that the overlaps between funding for disaffection, SEN, traveller support and so on can be minimised, is yet to be seen; but this would go some way to bridging the gap between the Government's agenda on social inclusion and inclusion for SEN.

Balance is also required in the area of devolved budgets for pupils at Stage 3 of the *Code of Practice*. Too much delegation of support services to individual schools may reduce the ability of the authority to make a 'specialist' contribution. Similarly, in the context of school improvement, it may weaken its ability to challenge schools. Devolution to a cluster or group of schools on the basis of an agreed menu of development towards inclusive practice may be a better option. A recent unpublished report on good practice in deploying support services (Cornwall, 1999) suggests that some of these issues can be made less contentious if the following are observed:

- clearly defining the purposes and objectives of support and outreach;

- support services and schools (mainstream and special) seen as part of a whole service and not separate domains in themselves;

- overall service management, providing a stronger basis to maximise efficiency;

- using pupil data on academic and social progress to evaluate services;

- clear performance indicators and quality control mechanisms.

Achieving equity of distribution

Having looked briefly at the nature of need and the type of support required to meet it, it is necessary to devise a mechanism whereby resources can be distributed equitably. Rightly, there is also pressure for local authorities to be cost-effective and efficient in the way they distribute public money, and this will require that they have clear and transparent methods of allocating funds that are perceived by parents and schools as fair. Arriving at and agreeing criteria, however, is a complex business, complicated further by the nature of support. Even if the local authority wishes to delegate the majority of its resources to schools, it will need to have a view about how those resources are best used; otherwise it cannot guarantee value for money.

As local authorities move more towards funding schools in partnership with other agencies, rather than individual pupils, in pursuance of a policy of inclusion, so schools will need to place less reliance on identifying individual pupil need and concentrate more on addressing whole school issues that arise out of planning for diversity. Further, if the local authority wishes to promote this through a broader definition of need it will need to find alternative methods of funding to those which require a headcount of individual pupils at each stage of the *Code of Practice*. We need to develop a method of funding that inverts the funnel, so to speak, one that not only reduces the perverse incentive but also moves current resources back towards emerging need. Such a method would also be more in keeping with the Government's intentions on early intervention. The major problem, of course, is that the *Code of Practice*, with its accumulative stages of resource allocation, does not easily support such a shift in emphasis.

The development of explicit criteria for allocating resources has two purposes. The first, to demonstrate equity and fairness. The second, to regulate the flow of funds. Local education authorities are at a distinct disadvantage when compared with Health and Social Services. For the most part, these two partners can distribute resources on a combination of eligibility and priority and, providing they can demonstrate fairness and the appropriate use of funds, constrain spending to the budget allocated.

The *1996 Education Act*, however, perpetuates the myth that demand-led resource allocation will be restricted to a notional 2% of the school population but it is difficult to maintain the concept of needs-led funding outside of a national set of eligibility criteria. In a context where there is unlikely to be continuing growth in SEN funding, more emphasis will need to be placed on the fairer distribution of what is available rather than on reinforcing perceptions of overall insufficiency.

A key question for the future, therefore, is what impact will the Government's national strategies for literacy and numeracy have on the level of pupils registered as SEN, and will this of itself reduce referrals to statutory assessment? Logic would dictate that it should, but to what degree? Should more resources be directed away from SEN to support whole school strategies for teaching key skills? If the answer is yes, then more money will need to be moved from SEN dedicated funding into the pupil formula with a clear set of regarding standards.

The perverse incentive

I turn now to the so-called 'perverse incentive'. Generally described, it is the process by which schools receive their allocation of funding at the school-based stages of the *Code of Practice* based on an aggregation of individual pupil need. There are a number of ways of arriving at this but all methods depend on 'banding' levels of need, and hence support, and most rely on schools identifying pupils within a range of educational indicators, usually referred to as 'descriptors'. The school's budget is based on a moderated profile of need in which particular levels of need represent a percentage of the school roll. Some systems also incorporate proxy measures. Most are referred to as 'an audit'.

Each year Kent has consulted head teachers on the continued use and/or modification of the SEN Audit. Each year a large majority of schools support its continuation. A favourable interpretation of this would suggest that schools recognise that the audit supports their efforts to identify and respond to pupils with special educational needs and that it is consistent with the SEN *Code of Practice*. A more cynical interpretation would be that schools see it as a way of raising much needed additional finance. The main argument against this form of funding, therefore, is escalating cost. Similarly, if schools are responding to the 'incentive' to identify needs by placing pupils on the SEN register unnecessarily, then they are also promoting children to higher stages of the Code and consequently fuelling an increase in statutory assessments. This argument appears to assume that schools do not have sufficient integrity to operate this system, although an alternative observation would be that schools care sufficiently about their pupils to want to maximise whatever resources are available.

The term 'perverse incentive', then, is sometimes used to discredit methods of funding that are needs driven, and this is part of a larger campaign to prevent ever-increasing proportions of budgets being allocated to pupils with SEN. A more important argument, however, is that in providing a financial incentive to identify pupil need, schools will be encouraged to view the meeting of needs as 'in addition' to normal activity. Pupils with SEN may then be viewed as an extra burden and not their responsibility. This is a more compelling argument in the context of inclusion. It is clearly not helpful to have a system of funding whereby it may be in the schools' interests to demonstrate lack of pupil achievement in order to gain more resources. Whilst the evidence does not necessarily support the view that schools are deliberately inflating children's difficulties, it does seem that they are ratifying failure or lack of progress rather than concentrating on reviewing interventions to see if these are appropriate. Further, it is not always evident that sufficient detailed attention has been given to whether the pupil's level of progress is acceptable relative to his/her starting points and particular needs. Inclusive practice, therefore, demands a different and more positive approach.

If the wider concept of 'educational need' is accepted as a more appropriate way of supporting groups of schools, then it will also be necessary to find a method of funding that recognises the social inclusion issues that this implies. Clearly a return to free school meals as a proxy indicator is not enough. Whilst it is possible to demonstrate a global correlation between this indicator and incidence of need in some authorities, at the school and cluster level the correlation is much less pronounced. One of the strengths of the SEN Audit is that it does unify the system of funding between the school-based and statutory-based stages of the *Code of Practice*. In devising alternative methods, it will be necessary to retain this element of continuity.

Alternatives

For schools with 'high levels of educational need', there are a variety of possibilities based on verifiable environmental factors such as the 'z score' index, post code, child-protection data, dental service data, crime statistics, casual admissions, numbers of pupils registered as in need of support for English as additional language. Some of these statistics may be as easy to collect as free school meals and reflect more accurately the global needs of a group or cluster of schools. They will, however, require multi-agency involvement and eventually some form of harmonised database, but this in turn may provide the necessary basis for joint-funding, particularly in the early years. Whatever the choice, there will be an overriding requirement to ensure that funding remains predictable year on year; a principle not always achieved by an audit. Given that some of these factors could be used in the production of a formula, the next requirement is to produce a mechanism that fairly reflects the range of special educational needs that lie within the broader umbrella of educational need. This mechanism will need to have embedded within it the ability for schools to demonstrate value added through a reduction in the number of pupils moving to 'support plus' or statutory assessment. More importantly, from the wider school improvement perspective, it will need to demonstrate improved educational outcomes.

One such approach is to use a modified version of baseline assessment. I suggest modified because it would be possible to extend baseline assessment downwards towards the pre-school years, linking the early assessments made by other agencies with educational objectives. Some measure of consistency has already been achieved in this area through the introduction of Desirable Learning Outcomes. Community needs could then be considered by the whole group of schools, and more so if these groupings or clusters were aligned to admission forums. The admission forum would then be clearer about the support needs required across the group of schools at a very early stage, both at pre-school and secondary transfer.

A further advantage would be the ability to feed this information into the comparative data already issued to schools by LEAs, enabling them to demonstrate value added and genuine improvement. It may even be used to set targets for reducing the number of pupils registered as SEN. Educational achievement might then be used as a prime indicator of inclusive practice.

If such an approach were adopted, it would be necessary to ensure that the processes used for statutory assessment reflected the same broad principles. This could be done, and indeed is being done in a number of LEAs, through greater delegation of the 'Statement support budget' to schools. This is most successfully achieved at present at the level of the secondary school where the economies of scale allow for some form of service level agreement to be made between the school and the LEA regarding a global budget to cover all Statement needs. This sometimes carries with it tolerance levels whereby the school absorbs the cost of further statutory assessments and likewise retains funds if the number of Statements reduce. Where this has been tried on a trial basis in Kent, it has met with some success, but evaluation suggests that it operates more effectively where management systems for staff deployment and supervision are more secure. Longstanding evidence from Nottinghamshire and elsewhere suggests that it would be possible to translate this into primary schools through a process of cluster management.

Two further issues would then need to be considered. First, Statements should be written in a way that facilitates a more direct assessment of outcomes through the annual review procedure. Tighter criteria for 'entitlement' to statutory assessment might help here but in the medium term there will be a need to rescind a proportion of Statements and this will require a sharper description of the expected outcomes. Second, a way will need to be found to describe individual pupil needs at Stage 3 (Support Plus) and statutory assessment which is less prone to categorisation.

Whether one can actually profile a child's needs and define the additional and different support required without resorting to some form of labelling for the purposes of funding remains to be seen. Some form of audit approach at this level may still be required. This was clearly the case for the Further Education Funding Council (FEFC), recently, when considering how best to introduce consistency and equity of funding for students placed in independent colleges, post-16. Having given full regard to the recommendations of the Tomlinson Report, and having recognised that students should not be labelled, they have accepted the advice of Cooper-Lybrand and introduced an Audit, which in shape and character is similar to the original SEN Audit first used in Kent in 1988. The rationale is the same; namely, that in order for the college to have sufficient resources to respond to particular pupil needs it will require a budget that reflects individual support requirements. The FEFC has concluded it cannot do this without introducing a degree of global categorisation against required 'levels of support' for specific aspects of need. It may be the case, therefore, that some degree of compromise will be required which allows some funding to be distributed at the higher levels of need utilising descriptors for individual pupils, albeit distributing the aggregate funding to a cluster for the purposes of devolved management.

Perhaps a clearer definition of what categories are meant to achieve might help here, relating them more to funding principles than individual children or special school designation. Again, Crowther et al (1998) have something to offer in the way that they have approached the redefinition of MLD through individual profiles. They begin with different levels of achievement within the National Curriculum; defining two groups within this, milder and more severe. They then go on to 'add' particular characteristics around emotional/behavioural needs and physical/sensory.

They end up with six descriptions that they suggest help to define outcomes across a range of domains concerned with academic, affective, life-chance and schooling processes. This approach could help in the reorientation away from 'needs' towards locally managed, aggregate budgets that deal more with outcomes - perhaps linking it to the more recent work of the NFER on target setting for SEN.

One further possibility may lie in the development of 'inclusive indicators'. Why not fund at least part of the school budget on indicators associated with such practices as:

- teaching of study skills and self-help strategies;

- a well-ordered and clearly labelled environment to encourage independent working;

- a broader class/whole school role for LSAs;

- target setting for all pupils;

- curriculum planning that takes account of learning styles and makes clear reference to extension materials and teaching approaches;

- training opportunities for staff and parents;

- the inclusive/exclusive nature of the SENCO role;

- the manner in which external agencies are used;

- the views of the children?

This is only a tentative list. A great deal of work would need to be done to verify these types of outcomes as well as the aggregate achievement referred to earlier.

One can see, therefore, an approach to funding beginning to emerge which is more consistent with the Government's aim of furthering inclusion and which better suits the climate of school improvement and school accountability for individual pupil achievement. Whilst the 11 principles outlined by Ingrid Lunt and Jennifer Evans remain important, time has moved on and we must now take account of the issues and tensions which arise from inclusion, and in particular:

- a broader view of educational need and social inclusion;

- greater multi-agency involvement, particularly in the pre-school and early years;

- 'project-based' and 'integrated' service support, which includes special schools;

- monitoring against clearly defined affective and social outcomes as well as academic standards;

- promoting positive motivators to improve pupil performance;

- the redefinition of, and use made of, categories or educational descriptors.

None of this can go forward, however, until local authorities have a clearer view of what inclusion means and have set objectives to which they can align resources.

Conclusion

Funding to promote inclusion, then, is a complex business. The purpose of this paper has been to raise issues for discussion and hopefully, on the way, point to some tentative solutions.

References

Ainscow, M., Farrell, P., Tweddle, D. and Malki, G. (1999) *Effective Practice in Inclusion and in Special and Mainstream Schools Working Together*. London: Department for Education and Employment.

Cornwall, J. (1999) *Models of good practice in funding and delivering tuition support services, including an evaluation of strengths and weaknesses using comparisons between different LEA models*. Unpublished, LEA commissioned, report. Canterbury: Cornwall.

Crowther, D., Dyson, A. and Millward, A. (1998) *Costs and Outcomes for Pupils with Moderate Learning Difficulties in Special and Mainstream Schools*. London: Department for Education and Employment.

Department for Education (1994) *The Code of Practice on the Identification and Assessment of Special Educational Needs.* London: HMSO.

Department for Education and Employment (1998) *Meeting Special Educational Needs: A Programme of Action.* London: HMSO.

Department for Education and Employment (1997) *Excellence for All Children: Meeting Special Educational Needs.* London: HMSO.

Evans, J. and Lunt, I. (1994) *Allocating Resources for Special Educational Needs Provision.* Special Educational Needs Policy Steering Group, Policy Paper 4. Tamworth: National Association for Special Educational Needs (NASEN).

Gray, P. (1998) *Resourcing for Children with Special Educational Needs in New Kent.* Unpublished report commissioned by Kent County Council. Maidstone: KCC.

Housden, P. (1993) *Bucking the Market: LEAs and Special Needs.* Special Educational Needs Policy Steering Group, Policy Paper 1. Tamworth: National Association for Special Educational Needs (NASEN).

National Association for Special Educational Needs (1998) *Policy document on SEN funding.* Tamworth: NASEN.

Norwich, B. (1999) Review Article 'Special or inclusive education?' *European Journal of Special Educational Needs Education*, 14, 1, 90-96.

Warnock Report (1978) *Special Educational Needs.* London: HMSO.

Chapter 3
Discussants' papers
1. Funding and inclusion

DR COR J. W. MEIJER, Staff member of the European Agency for Development of Special Needs Education

Introduction*

Almost every country supports the view that children with special needs should be educated in the mainstream. Countries do not succeed in achieving this in the same successful way. Research shows that countries differ in terms of the number of students with special needs that are integrated. Major differences have been described not only in quantitative terms, but also in terms of educational organisation and the actual provisions for special needs students in regular education. Recently, the focus is on a capital factor in realising inclusive education: educational funding. More specifically, a strong link is assumed between funding of special needs education and the inclusion models developed and implemented in education.

Framework

The report of the European Agency for Development of Special Needs Education on the 'Provision for Pupils with Special Educational Needs' (Meijer, 1998) revealed that European countries have quite different approaches towards the education of pupils with special educational needs. Some countries segregate high proportions of their pupils in special schools or special classes. Other countries educate only small proportions of SEN pupils in a separate provision. These differences, which may vary between less than 1% and more than 5%, are the result of many factors. These factors have been extensively addressed in studies of different organisations and (research) institutes. Researchers pointed at the differences in history, policy, demographic and geographical factors, but also on different societal views about handicapped and disabled people and the resulting approaches in provision for them.

Thus, several factors are responsible for variation in 'inclusionary' practices within and between countries. As pointed out, recently attention

---

* This text is partly based on the report of the European Agency for Development in Special Needs Education '*Financing of special needs education. A seventeen country study of the relation between financing of special needs education and integration*' (Meijer, 1999)

has been given to another relevant factor in realising inclusive education: the way education and more specifically special needs education is funded. It is hypothesised that funding largely determines the types of provision that have been developed and implemented. Thus, it is assumed that the system of funding influences the integration or segregation of students with special needs in education. On the basis of data of 17 European countries, that is all the member countries of the European Agency for Development in Special Needs Education, an analysis is made of the different funding systems and of the impact of financing on inclusion. The results that are presented here are based on that study. The final report of the study will be available by the end of 1999.

In thinking about funding regulations all sorts of topics need to be considered. Funding systems affect the flexibility of schools to make special provision, may necessitate formal identification procedures, may create bureaucracy, raise questions of accountability and (budget) control, affect the position of parents and may require the need for decentralisation of decision-making processes. Each model of funding of special needs provision is expected to have certain positive outcomes. Funding based on lump-sum models seems more flexible and avoids bureaucratic procedures; pupil-bound budget empowers the parents, stimulates accountability and results in equal access to appropriate education. However, all these different funding systems may also result in negative consequences. New funding systems will always be a compromise between all these aspects. In the following we explore a number of these compromises.

Parameters in funding models

Every existing or newly developed funding model can be described with a set of parameters, for example: the sort of resources (time, money, materials, training facilities), the destination for the resources (parents/pupils, schools, communities, regional institutions), earmarking of the resources (yes or no), group or individual-based funding, the conditions for funding and the degrees of freedom in expenditure (advance budget or declaration based).

Here, we confine ourselves to the most relevant parameters concerning special education funding: destination locus (who gets the funds) and the conditions for funding, which we discuss below.

Destination locus

Generally, this parameter is important in discussions about inclusion. In principle the funds can be allocated in many different ways. In the first place they can be allocated to the clients of the educational system: the pupils and/or parents. Also schools can receive funding. In this respect there are two options: special schools or regular schools. Another possibility is to allocate funds to groups of schools or other regional institutions like school advisory centres. Finally funds can be delegated to municipalities or regions.

Funding indicators

Three main categories of indicators are usually distinguished: input, throughput and output. Input-funding is when the funding is based, for example, on the determined need of each of the destination levels, like the number of special needs children in a school, municipality or region. Inputs may also be defined in terms of referral rates, low achievement scores, number of disadvantaged children and so on. The key point is that funding is based on (expressed or measured) needs.

The second model, throughput-funding, is based on the functions or tasks that have to be undertaken or developed. It is not based on needs but the services provided by a school, municipality or region. Finances are allocated on the condition of developing and maintaining certain services. Schools, municipalities or regions are equally treated: funds are based on total enrolment or on other population indicators. Of course, in this model certain conditions in terms of output can be explicated, but the funding itself is not based on outputs (nor inputs). Also control and accountability can play an important role here, as with the other funding models.

In the third option, funds are allocated on the basis of output: for example, in terms of the number of referred children (the lower the number, the more funds) or achievement scores (added value: the higher the achievement scores, the more funds). The output can be defined on different aggregation levels, as pointed out before.

It is clear that these three models have extremely different incentives. A needs-based system entails a bonus on having or formulating needs, an output-based system generates behaviour towards achieving the desired results, and the throughput model does not reinforce inputs or outputs but tries to generate services. Furthermore, the three models may have their own negative co-effects as well as unexpected or expected strategic behaviour. For example, an output model may reinforce the referral of children with expected low gains in achievement scores to other parts of the system. On the other hand, input funding on the basis of low achievement reinforces low achievement itself: more funds can then be expected. Throughput funding may reinforce inactivity: whether anything is done or not, funds will be available. Combination of different indicators is also possible. Throughput financing can be combined with output control, for example. Low outputs may then be used as a possible correction on the throughput budget for a following period of time.

On the basis of these two parameters it is possible to describe the funding systems in the different countries and to discuss the pros and cons of these. This will be done in the next section.

Funding models

Throughout the 17 countries of Europe different models of financing of special education can be recognised. However, it is impossible to group the participating countries in a few clear categories. In most countries different funding models are used simultaneously for different groups of special needs pupils. Also, within the strongly decentralised countries, different funding models are used by the regional authorities. Finally, the funding of integrated services is usually different from the funding of the special provision in separate settings and it is therefore impossible to characterise a country by one simple formula or funding system. As a result, the discussion about the different funding models is not based on comparisons between countries but on comparisons of models. Below, countries are mentioned alongside different funding models, but this should not be interpreted as trying to highlight the countries' main funding model but as an illustration of the place where the specific model can be found.

The first model is the model that is currently used in countries with a relatively high proportion of children in segregated settings and in which special schools are financed by the central government on the basis of the number of pupils with special needs and the severity of the disability. This model can typically be described as a needs-based funding model on the level of the special school. In terms of our theoretical framework this model is an 'input' model: the degree of the need forms the basis of the financing. Governments pay special schools on the basis of their needs. The indicator for 'need' is here the number of pupils with special needs. The decision-making processes are mostly organised by regional or school-based commissions. The countries that work with this type of 'input-based funding on (special) school level' are: Austria, Belgium (both Flemish and French Community), France, Germany, Ireland and the Netherlands. Also in countries with relatively low percentages of children in special schools or classes a central needs-based model for the financing of special schools may be used. In, for example, Luxembourg, Spain and Sweden (at least a small part of) the special school system is paid by the central government on the basis of the number of children and their disabilities.

28

A second model is the model in which the central government allocates the funds to municipalities via a lump sum (with possible corrections for socio-economic differences) and where the municipality has the main responsibility for dividing the funds to lower levels. The first step can be characterised by a 'throughput model': funds are allocated to municipalities independent of the number of children with special needs within those municipalities. In the second step needs-based indicators can be used, but also other types of allocation processes may be used. Countries that focus strongly on this type of decentralised special needs funding are Denmark, Finland, Greece, Iceland, Norway and Sweden. Here, municipalities decide about the way in which special education funds should be used and about the degree of funding. In Denmark, Iceland, Norway and Sweden the following principle is embedded in the funding system: the more funds municipalities put in separate provision as special schools or special classes, the less is available for integrated services.

Within the countries where this model can be found, school support centres generally play a decisive role in the allocation procedures (for example, in Denmark and Norway).

As pointed out before, different indicators and procedures can be used within the allocation processes from municipalities to schools: in some countries also in this stage 'throughput-models' are used (Sweden, for example: some municipalities allocate the special education funds to schools irrespective of the needs of those schools). But mostly an indicator for need is used in this stage of the process as well.

In the third model the financing is not delegated to municipalities but to a higher level of aggregation such as provinces, counties, prefectures, school clusters and so on. In this model the central government funds special education indirectly through other layers where the main responsibility lies for special provision. Examples of countries that use this model are Denmark (for the more severe special needs), France (for integrated services), Greece and Italy. In the Netherlands it has recently been introduced for the milder special needs: the funds for these pupils are allocated to school clusters on the basis of a throughput-model: clusters that consist of regular and special schools receive funds for special provision irrespective of the number of pupils with special needs.

In England and Wales the responsibility is being laid at the local authority level and the local authority decides on the level of funding it will make available to meet its statutory responsibilities towards pupils with special educational needs.

29

In some countries funds are tied to pupils: the budget for special education is based on the type of disability and parents can in principle choose where they want to have their child educated. This model of pupil-bound budget can be found in Austria (for the certified children), England and Wales (statement-procedure), France (the so-called SEA-procedure) and Luxembourg. The system is foreseen to be introduced in the Netherlands (for the more severe needs). This model can be described as an input or needs-based model on pupil level. The more needs the child has, the more funds are connected to him or her.

In a few countries, authorities base (part of) the funding of special education on the belief or assumption that (milder) forms of special needs are evenly spread over schools. Some other countries believe that every mainstream needs a certain amount of (earmarked) special needs funding in order to serve these pupils adequately. In these countries, the funding of (mainstream) schools consists of a fixed budget for special needs education irrespective of the number of children with special needs in those schools. This model, at least this part of the finance-model for special education, can be characterised as throughput-funding on school level. Examples of countries where these approaches to the funding of milder forms of special needs can be found are Austria (fixed budget based on the total number of children in a school), Denmark (some municipalities) and Sweden (some municipalities). In the Netherlands this throughput-model is currently being used for the funding of special education (for the milder forms of special needs) on school cluster level.

The European Agency study of the financing of special needs education in the member countries reveal that funding models are developing strongly. In some countries huge changes are to be expected or have recently been implemented. In the Netherlands both the funding of the provision for milder special needs and the provision for the more severe needs are and will be drastically changed. The input-based model on school level (a special school is funded according to the number of pupils in that school) will be replaced by a throughput-model for the milder special needs (through the funding of school clusters, which has already been implemented) and an input model on pupil level: the pupil-bound budget. In Austria, the pupil-bound budget system is currently being debated; the model of pupil-bound budgets is held responsible for the undesired growth of labelling and special education budgets and as a hindrance for more emphasis on prevention.

Efficiency, effectiveness, strategic behaviour and accountability

The first clear result of the study is that in countries where the finance system is characterised by a direct input-funding model of special schools (more children in special schools, more funds), the most negative voices are heard. These countries (for example, Austria, the Netherlands, Belgium - both French and Flemish Community - and France) point at the different forms of strategic behaviour within the educational field (by parents, teachers or other actors). These forms of strategic behaviour may result in less integration, more labelling and a raising of costs. Much money is spent on such non-educational matters as litigation, diagnostic procedures and so on. It is not remarkable that these are in the group of countries with relatively higher percentages of children with special needs in separate settings. Quite strongly, some of these countries report that the finance system influences their integration policy negatively! For some countries (the Netherlands, for example) this finding is the main reason for changing the finance system of special needs education drastically.

Also, other countries report forms of strategic behaviour. These forms of strategic behaviour can be summarised as follows:

- parents want as much funds for their special needs child as possible;

- also (special and mainstream) schools want as much funds as possible;

- however, schools generally prefer the funds for the less difficult-to-handle pupils.

A second finding is that countries that have a strong decentralised system where the municipality has the main responsibility for the organisation of special education generally report positive effects of their systems. Countries like Norway, Sweden, Finland and Denmark mention almost no negative side-effects of their systems and are generally very satisfied with their finance systems. Systems where the municipalities decide on the basis of information about school support or advising centres, and where the allocation of more funds to separate settings directly influences the amount of funds for mainstream schools, seem to be very effective in terms of achieving integration.

A negative view is also heard from these strongly decentralised countries: regional differences can be quite strong, and as a result the circumstances can differ for parents of children with special educational needs. However, decentralisation is seen generally as an important prerequisite for integration. Countries such as Sweden, France and Norway state this more or less explicitly. It is exactly this argument that stimulates the debate for more decentralisation in Germany as well.

Pupil-bound budgeting as used in Austria seems to have some clear disadvantages as well. Sometimes mainstream schools are eager to have these children (and their budgets) within their walls in order to be able to split the existing classes into smaller ones. However, it is likely that they prefer children (with budgets) who do not cause them too much additional work. Also, parents will always try to get the best for their child and as a result will try to get the highest amounts of special needs funding. This pupil-bound budget system is certainly not advisable for children with milder special needs. Criteria for learning disabilities are vague, ambiguous and changing over time and this in itself may be a source of debate if budgets are linked to children. In practice, only clear-cut criteria are useful if funds are tied to children. If it is not possible to develop these, pupil-bound budgets should not be used. Generally it is desirable that funds are spent on special education itself (in an inclusive setting), instead of on bureaucratic procedures like diagnosis, categorisation, appeals and litigation.

Concerning the issue of accountability, it should be noted that in none of the member countries is it common that schools have to report what they have achieved with their special education budgets. Although in some countries inspections are quite ordinary, these are mostly concerned with the efforts of schools concerning educational arrangements and matters, but rarely with the output of these efforts. The focus is mostly on the type of arrangements and interventions and the way they are carried out, but never on the results that have been achieved. Generally, the evaluation and monitoring procedures within countries should be improved also within the framework of special education. In the first place it is important to guarantee and to stimulate an efficient and effective spending of public funds. Secondly, it seems necessary to show the clients of the educational systems (pupils with special needs and their parents) that education within the mainstream setting (including all the additional facilities and support) is of a sufficiently high quality. It seems that earmarking of special education funds, forms of control, monitoring and evaluation form inherent elements of an adequate finance system on the field of special education.

Indeed, the study revealed that financing of special needs education is one of the best explanatory factors of the integration-segregation continuum. If funds are not allocated in line with an explicit inclusionary policy, inclusion is unlikely to be realised in practice. That is clearly demonstrated in this study. The mechanisms of financing can explain discrepancies between general policies on inclusive education and the practical organisation of inclusion. In fact, financing could be regarded as one of the most important factors that may contribute to the further development of inclusive practices.

There are a few lines alongside which improvement of the finance of special education may be undertaken. On the basis of this study the following recommendations can be made:

1. A so-called throughput-model at the regional (municipality) level seems to be the most attractive option, especially if some elements of output funding are incorporated. In such a model budgets for special needs are delegated at central level to regional institutions (municipalities, districts, school clusters). At regional level it is decided how the money is spent and which pupils should profit from the special services. It is desirable that the institution that decides on the allocation of special needs budgets has or can make use of (independent) expertise in the area of special needs and the tools to implement and maintain strategies and services related to this.

2. Inclusion can be achieved more easily in a decentralised model when compared to a central approach. In a centrally prescribed plan too much emphasis may be put on the organisational characteristics of that specific model without inclusionary practice being realised in practice. Local organisations with some autonomy may be far better equipped to change the system. Therefore, a decentralised model is likely to be more cost-effective and provide fewer opportunities for undesirable forms of strategic behaviour. Nevertheless, the central government has to clearly specify which goals must be achieved. Decisions concerning the way in which such goals are to be achieved are then left to local organisations.

3. An important concern in a decentralised system is the issue of accountability. Clients of the education system and taxpayers in general have a right to know how funds are spent and to what end. Accordingly, some kind of monitoring, inspection and evaluation procedures will be inevitable elements of the funding system. The need for monitoring and evaluation is even greater in a decentralised model compared to more centralised options. Independent evaluation of the quality of education for children with special needs is therefore part of such a model.

References

Meijer, C. J. W., Pijl, S. J. and Hegarty, S. (Eds.) (1994) *New perspectives in special education. A six country study of integration.* London: Routledge.

Meijer, C. J. W. (1998) *Integration in Europe: Provision for Pupils with Special Educational Needs*. Middelfart, European Agency for Development in Special Needs Education.

Meijer, C. J. W., Pijl, S. J. and Waslander, S. (1999) *Special Education Funding and Integration*. In J. G. Chambers, T. B. Parrish and C. M. Guarino (Eds) *Funding Special Education* (pp. 63-85). Thousands Oaks, CA: Corwin Press, Inc.

Meijer, C. J. W. (in press). *Funding of special needs education. A seventeen country study of the relation between financing of special needs education and integration*. Middelfart, European Agency for Development in Special Needs Education.

Pijl, S. J., Meijer, C. J. W. and Hegarty, S. (Eds) (1997) *Inclusive education: A global agenda*. London: Routledge.

2. Discussion comments

PROFESSOR KLAUS WEDELL, Emeritus Professor of Educational Psychology (special educational needs)

John Moore has provided us with a very comprehensive treatment of the key issues. It is particularly helpful that he sets his points in the context of the development of policy since the previous policy seminar on this topic held in 1994, in the wake of the *1993 Education Act* introduced by the previous Government. This Act promoted competition between schools, and constrained the role of LEAs - both policies which jeopardised the ways in which children's special educational needs could be met.

I just want to add comments on two issues:

- the potential impact which the present Government's policies can have on the concept of special educational provision;

- the context of decisions about the allocation of resources to meet special educational needs.

Policy impacts on the concept of special educational provision. I will briefly mention two points:

1. There is no doubt that the present Government has moved towards inclusion, as indicated by the Secretary of State's resolve in the Green Paper, that 'we shall promote the inclusion of children with SENs within mainstream schooling wherever possible.' Although the final clause limits the scope of his statement, it does alter the implications of the qualified right to inclusion as expressed in the wording of the current legislation. We are now called to account about:

- why a child's needs cannot be met in schools,

- why this cannot be achieved without interfering with other children's education,

- why inclusion cannot be compatible with the efficient use of resources.

However, as John Moore points out, the Manchester University research found that LEAs were still very unclear about how they understood the concept of inclusion.

35

2. The concept of 'generally made provision' has been altered by a number of the Government's initiatives. These have been intended to make an impact on many of the problems facing schools and their pupils, including many aspects which are related to special educational needs. Both the Literacy and the Numeracy Strategies present a more detailed curricular progression, within which teaching should be matched more closely to the diversity of individual pupils' learning needs. The recommendations about grouping pupils probably represents the first instance of guidance about matching the grouping of pupils to the specific pedagogical demands of what is to be learned. Similarly, the requirement on LEAs to be the lead agency in developing a Behaviour Support Policy in their area has the potential for creating a spectrum of support for pupils' behaviour problems, particularly in mainstream schools. In addition, many of the Education Action Zones (EAZs) are developing provision which is also directed at greater effectiveness in teaching and learning.

These initiatives have a potentially positive impact on the 'situated difficulties in learning' to which John Moore refers in Brahm Norwich's writing. However, set against this positive influence, we should not underestimate the countervailing impact on schools of the Government's target-setting policies, and on LEAs of the 'Fair Funding' policies. The former tend to push schools into expediency to increase assessment results, rather than to an equitable allocation of resources for support. The latter limit LEAs' capacity to fund support services - and even limit their capacity to check on whether mainstream schools are using their allocated resources to provide effective support to meet pupils' special educational needs.

The context of decisions about the allocation of resources

John Moore rightly points to LEAs' dilemmas in allocating funds to meet pupils' special educational needs. LEAs have finite resources, and so are faced with the choice between the alternatives of increasing the 'generally made' provision, or of maintaining more resources to allocate to pupils on assessments of individual need. This dilemma is inherently unresolvable. My feeling is that LEA officers and school senior management have often taken upon themselves a greater degree of responsibility for making these decisions than is appropriate. I will illustrate this view in relation to three points.

1. In my opinion, it seems far more appropriate that both LEA administrators and school senior management teams should pass the dilemma about these decisions back to their democratic constituencies. For example,

LEAs could set up specifically constituted consultative groups of representatives from the parent bodies of children with special educational needs, to whom they could refer for views on resource allocation policies - and some LEAs have begun to do this. Similarly, schools' senior managements should be far more willing to involve their governing bodies to share openly in making these decisions, particularly now that there is increased parent representation.

2. The present Government has stressed the importance of 'joined-up' thinking between the various statutory agencies in meeting needs. The necessity for cross-service collaboration has, of course, long been recognised. The majority of the Government's initiatives now include a requirement for this kind of collaboration, but as before, it is still taking a long time to materialise. To some extent the problem lies with the central Government departments themselves, in so far as these are not setting a good example.

For the LEA, is it important that it has a clear understanding about how the responsibility to meet pupils' special educational needs has to be shared out between services. The perennial problem of the provision of speech therapy services is an example. In one EAZ, there has been an initiative whereby EAZ funding is allocated to enabling speech therapists to work in the infant departments of primary schools to carry out preventative work. This involves collaboration with the LEA learning support service, to help teachers to identify and respond to children who are delayed in their language comprehension and expression. In the same EAZ, there is joint funding to pay for social services personnel to take part in the work of schools' parent centres. It is intended that the evaluation of these projects will demonstrate the benefit for the three services to continue such joint funding when the present EAZ resources cease.

3. One of the greatest problems facing LEAs in allocating resources to schools to meet pupils' special educational needs, is how to ensure that the allocation matches the different needs of individual schools - and is flexible in responding to the changing needs within schools. It is generally recognised that LEAs can only approximate to this goal - both because the criteria for allocation to individual schools are too crude, and because the systems for allocation are too rigid over time.

Colleagues and I have found (Evans, Lunt, Wedell and Dyson, 1999) that some LEAs have moved towards reducing this problem, by allocating a proportion of special needs resources to groupings of schools which are collaborating both within and across phase. It is then up to the groupings of schools to share the resources between themselves. This delegation enables the LEA to allocate a more substantial amount to the school groupings. These, in turn, then have the opportunity to achieve strategic planning, economies of scale and flexibility in sharing the resources between the participating schools. For example, in one pyramid of small rural schools, none of the individual schools could afford to appoint an appropriately qualified special needs co-ordinator. The schools therefore decided jointly to create a post for a full-time teacher with appropriate expertise, who could serve all the five schools, and also could ensure more effective transition from the primary to the secondary school. Needless to say, such collaboration also has its obligation on schools to develop a degree of mutual trust in arriving at decisions about the provision and its management. These pressures obviously increase when funding becomes constrained. However, as we found in our research, such trust is achievable.

This example illustrates the need to match resource decisions to a level of specificity which corresponds to the scope for cost-effective allocation. The Government's proposal in *Meeting Special Educational Needs: A Programme for Action*, to establish regional collaboration between LEAs to provide special schools for minority special needs, is a similar instance but at a wider level of sharing.

I have tried to point to two aspects of the topic of this seminar which are either changing, or have the potential to change, some of the issues which face us in the concern to develop inclusive policies. The first aspect involves the well-known risk of gaps between policy and its implementation. More seriously perhaps, it illustrates the potential conflicts between separate government policies. The second aspect relates to the context within which resource allocation decisions are made. The points I have made suggest that there is scope for a sharing of responsibility for decisions, which can lead to greater effectiveness in using resources.

Reference

Department for Education and Employment (1998) *Meeting Special Educational Needs: A Programme for Action.* London: HMSO.

Evans, J., Lunt, I., Wedell, K. and Dyson, A. (1999) *Collaborating for effectiveness: empowering schools to become inclusive.* Buckingham: Open University Press.

3. Resources, policies and educational practice

PROFESSOR PAUL CROLL and DR DIANA MOSES,
University of Reading

This brief response to John Moore's stimulating paper is organised into three sections. First, we want to highlight some aspects of the paper which we feel raise particularly important issues for developments in policy and practice related to inclusion. Second, we outline some findings from two recently completed ESRC-funded studies of special educational needs which we conducted at the University of Reading. Finally we bring these together and identify some implications of the Moore paper and of our research findings for policies which promote inclusion.

The discussion paper

Six aspects of the Moore paper to which we would particularly draw attention are presented below.

- The crucial link between issues of special educational needs and issues of school improvement and school development. We have argued elsewhere that, although the inclusion debate has been largely held in the special education community, inclusion is essentially an issue for mainstream rather than special education (Croll & Moses, 1999a). It is still very unclear whether the direction in which current policy is pushing school improvement is compatible with movements towards inclusion.

- Funding arrangements should be directed towards promoting change as well as towards efficient means of distributing resources. It is worth noting that funding mechanisms necessarily influence the direction of change whether or not they are intended to do so. Previous funding systems such as those associated with Statements and the stages of the *Code of Practice* have often had important but unintended consequences for special education provision.

- The conceptual link between special educational needs and special educational provision makes it essential to look at the concept of SEN as well as at funding mechanisms. The definition in both the Warnock Report and the 1981 legislation of SEN as needs beyond what is ordinarily provided means that the level of ordinary mainstream provision partly determines what is special (Moses, Hegarty & Jowett, 1988).

- The use of indicators of special educational needs and the 'perverse incentive' is a further example of the unintended consequences of funding mechanisms.

- The balance between delegated and centralised budgets and the extent to which LEAs can delegate budgets and yet still ensure that their statutory obligations are met. The operation of the Special Educational Needs Tribunal has made this a particularly acute problem for some LEAs.

- The important point made in the paper about the move away from characterising educational needs as 'special'. We shall return to this when we discuss some of our own research on the apparent increase in the incidence of SEN.

Some research evidence

We have recently completed two research studies relating to current developments in the field of special educational needs. The first of these was concerned with LEA policy making with regard to special educational needs and particularly with regard to the future of the segregated special school sector (Croll & Moses, 1998, 1999b). The second was concerned with special educational needs in mainstream primary schools and with changes over the past two decades (Croll & Moses, 1999c).

As Norwich (1997, 1999) has shown, the slow decrease in segregated placements through the 1980s and 1990s has been very uneven across different local education authorities with some achieving a considerable degree of progress towards inclusion while others have maintained or increased their level of special school placements. Our research has shown the considerable resilience of the special school sector and also that the slow pace of reduction in special school provision is not mainly a result of inertia. Although existing patterns of provision are obviously an important influence on policy, many LEAs which have shown little or no change in overall levels of special school provision have experienced considerable change involving school closures and mergers and the opening of new special schools.

The most salient finding of this study has been the key importance of a few highly committed and highly influential individuals in local-level policy making related to special educational needs and inclusion. The general 'climate of opinion' supportive of inclusion proved less important than strongly held views of a few people in key locations. Virtually all

LEAs have policy documents supporting the fullest possible inclusion and most people within special education support inclusion as an ideal (though often as an impractical one (Croll & Moses, 2000)). In those areas where a lot of progress towards inclusion has been made this climate of opinion has been less of a direct influence on policy but more a resource upon which key policy makers can draw.

The study also highlighted the importance of major policy initiatives in moving towards more inclusive patterns of provision. LEAs which had hoped that incremental approaches to change, characterised by a series of small steps, would eventually lead to substantial shifts in provision had typically experienced little real change. The 'small steps' approach had typically been overtaken by the pragmatic reality of meeting individual needs and in aggregate had achieved little. On the other hand, a few LEAs had undertaken both a radical review of provision and a major political initiative that was prepared to confront and overrule parental and other opposition. Such initiatives seem to be a necessary feature of substantial shifts towards inclusion.

As we argued above, inclusion is essentially a mainstream issue. In 1998 we conducted a large-scale interview survey in 48 mainstream primary schools involving interviews with the heads, SENCOs and 299 class teachers (Croll & Moses, 1999c). The survey repeated a study we had conducted in 1981 (Croll & Moses, 1985). The research showed that over a quarter of children in mainstream Key Stage 2 (7-11 year-olds) classrooms were on the Register of Special Educational Needs, an increase of nearly 40% in special educational needs as seen by schools and teachers since 1981. Nearly all of these children had learning difficulties. Schools varied very considerably in the proportions of pupils having special educational needs ranging from one school with less than 10% of pupils on the SEN Register to two schools with more than 50%. Despite this range, however, most schools were in the middle categories for SEN and there was no tendency for schools to polarise into those with and those without children with special educational needs. In that sense, SEN continues to be an issue for all schools and all teachers.

The extent of special educational needs in schools correlated very strongly with overall achievement levels as indicated by the Key Stage 2 SAT results. This underlines the point made in John Moore's paper about the continuity between meeting special educational needs and meeting educational needs more generally. The very strong (negative) association between achievement and SEN shows that it is not realistic to distinguish in most cases between special educational needs and low achievement.

Another very strong correlation is that between the extent of special educational needs in a school and the proportion of children eligible for free school meals. SEN, like achievement levels more generally, are strongly influenced by social deprivation. A consequence of this, and one which has important implications for resource allocation strategies, is that schools confronting the highest level of special needs are also those with high levels of other problems and with the least access to parental and other community resources. The exception to the correlation of the incidence of SEN in a school and free school meals and overall achievement is with regard to pupils with a Statement of special educational needs. This gives some support to the view that it is only at this level of difficulty that resources should be targeted at identified children.

Moore's paper quotes Lunt and Evans (1994) in arguing for the importance of 'transparency and clarity' in resource allocation for SEN. From the perspective of mainstream schools there is a long way to go in achieving this. Teachers were often extremely unclear about resourcing mechanisms and frequently, for example, did not know whether particular aspects of support came from school or LEA resources. Head teachers often complained about the clarity and accessibility of LEA procedures and there were several instances where the account given by head teachers in an LEA of resource allocation was very different from that given by LEA officers. Heads were also sometimes suspicious of their LEAs and thought, for example, that LEA procedures were a covert device to keep numbers of Statements down. The number of Statements was a source of tension between schools and LEAs in a way which emphasises the importance of considering the policy consequences of funding mechanisms. LEA officers were virtually unanimous in feeling that too many children were the subject of statements and wanted to exert a downward pressure on Statementing. But most heads and teachers wanted more Statements as a way of accessing resources and LEAs therefore experienced an upward pressure on Statementing from their schools.

Most primary school teachers do not at the moment regard inclusion as being an issue of central importance and the views they expressed tended to vary depending on how this issue was presented to them. The principle of an all-inclusive mainstream education system has made very little ground among teachers and both teachers and heads were almost unanimous in seeing a continued role for special schools. On the other hand, when asked about children with special educational needs currently in their classes, teachers usually felt that the mainstream class was the right placement. This was true of children with Statements as well as those on lower stages of the *Code of Practice* and teachers frequently emphasised the social benefits to the child of being in the mainstream class. There was, therefore, a good deal of inclusive practice in the schools in the study.

Concluding comments

From the discussion of policy issues and research evidence above we want to identify some points for further consideration. We have put these as a series of assertions but intend them to provoke discussion.

- Any attempt to use resource allocation as a means of promoting inclusion must address the question of the future of special schools. The evidence from our and other studies suggests that such provision will not simply disappear in response to developments elsewhere and that a continued special sector will continue to attract clients.

- A resource allocation procedure which depends on the identification of individual children will inevitably lead to complex and bureaucratic assessment procedures. Often these assessments have been related more to the function of releasing resources than to the function of providing educationally relevant assessments of children's needs.

- The link between inclusion and school development and school improvement is important but has generated many unresolved tensions. It is not clear that inclusiveness has become a criterion for regarding schools as improving or that there are resource incentives for schools to improve in this direction. National policy has not yet addressed the link between poverty, special educational needs and low achievement in some schools.

- The increasing expansion of the concept of special educational need to include about one in four children in mainstream schools is not helpful with regard to the educational provision for these children and is a distraction from an inclusive agenda. The proportion of children for whom an individualised model of resourcing is appropriate is very low: probably even fewer than those currently at Stage 5 of the *Code of Practice*.

Acknowledgement

The two research studies described here were supported by grants from the Economic and Social Research Council (ESRC).

References

Croll, P. and Moses, D. (1985) *One in Five*. London: Routledge and Kegan Paul.

Croll, P. and Moses, D. (1998) 'Pragmatism, Ideology and Educational Change: The Case of Special Educational Needs.' *British Journal of Educational Studies*, 46, 1, 11-25.

Croll, P. and Moses, D. (1999a) 'Mainstream Primary Teachers' Views on Inclusion.' Paper presented at the Annual Conference of the British Educational Research Association.

Croll, P. and Moses, D. (1999b) 'Continuity and Change in Special School Provision: Some Perspectives on Local Authority Policy Making.' *British Educational Research Journal*, 25, 5.

Croll, P. and Moses, D. (1999c) *Special Needs in the Primary School*. London: Cassell.

Croll, P. and Moses, D. (2000) 'Ideologies and Utopias: Education Professionals' Views on Inclusion.' *European Journal of Special Needs Education*, 15, 1.

Department for Education (1994) *The Code of Practice on the Identification and Assessment of Special Educational Needs*. London: HMSO.

Lunt, I. and Evans, J. (1994) *Allocating Resources for Special Educational Needs Provision: Special Educational Needs Policy Steering Group, Policy Paper 4*. Stafford: NASEN.

Moses, D., Hegarty, S. and Jowett, S. (1988) *Supporting Ordinary Schools*. Windsor: NFER-Nelson.

Norwich, B. (1997) *A Trend towards Inclusion*. Bristol: CSIE.

Norwich, B. (1999) *Inclusion, 1996-98 A Continuing Trend,* Bristol: CSIE.

Warnock Report (1978) *Special Educational Needs*. London: HMSO.

Chapter 4
Summary of discussion and conclusions

Discussion at the seminar was initially in small groups followed by the reporting of main points to the whole group. Peter Gray, who chaired the seminar on behalf of the Steering Group, suggested that small groups consider a number of key issues from the paper in the form of trying to resolve dilemmas. This took the form of 'how to … without …'. What follows is a summary of some of the main points which small groups reported back to the plenary.

One group restated the position that a system of individual resourcing was inimical to the principles of inclusion. This meant that Statements needed to go. However, they were aware that there were many steps on the way to achieving this outcome. The issues for this group included the questions of accountability and the protection of the delegated additional funding. Here the LEA was seen to have a key role in monitoring developments with the use of quality indicators. Local consultation was seen as essential to achieving this end, as was political commitment in the system. A model of clustering of schools was seen as important in change towards this outcome.

In the second group they focused on inclusion and asked the question of how to stop schools becoming penalised for being good with pupils having SEN. They recognised the tendency for parents of other children to want to take their children away from schools with more pupils having SEN. This called for a broadening of measures of what constituted quality in schooling. The social and affective aspects of learning and development needed stressing and it was asserted that value added analyses might refocus attention on what schools actually contributed to pupils' learning and development more widely defined. This focus on a holistic and rounded picture of schooling was contrasted with the current emphasis on league tables.

The third group also focused on inclusion and considered how to ensure that all schools will take responsibility for pupils with SEN and not opt out from this. It was felt that there were no single answers. For example, the experience in Hampshire was different from that in Kent over the use of SEN Audit. Schools needed to be recognised and rewarded in some way for taking on this responsibility. This included recognition for schools that enabled more children to move down the *Code of Practice* stages.

The fourth group considered the tension between good practice in effective and inclusive schools and the funding of individual pupils with SEN. Related to this is the question of how LEAs were to increase their funding of mainstream schools for SEN. One suggestion was that all special schools be funded centrally and not by LEAs. As the Government was committed to some special schools, even if fewer in number than currently existed, funding could come direct from the DfEE. This would remove the tension experienced by LEAs and leave them to develop their inclusive policies.

General discussion pursued some of the above points. It was pointed out in response to the last suggestion about central funding of special schools, that some LEAs had unified education budgets. These included the costs of transport and therapy. The principle was that money followed pupils and that it was not a good idea to have empty places in special schools. This meant that LEAs tell special schools that money would come and go depending on pupil numbers. It was pointed out, however, that this scheme threatened the continuity of provision in special schools. One Education Officer said that LEAs cannot underwrite the future of special schools. An example was given of an MLD special school where all the resources going to this school were redirected into mainstream. This raised further questions about the position of special schools teachers in such schools. Do they get retraining and is there any buffering of this change? One response was that the LEA could ensure that there were jobs for special schools teachers in the new system.

Another issue which was discussed was the systems of accountability between schools and LEAs. It was suggested that there is a need for work in developing systems of accountability. These might range from a light to a heavy touch system of accountability. Another important area was the issue of teaching and learning. There was a tendency for these crucial questions to be masked by blanket resource problems. It was asserted that parents knew what their children needed, what was critical was finding ways to meet these needs. Creativity was called for here.

In his final comments John Moore responded to many of the points that arose from his paper. He saw the need to find the appropriate level of resource allocation which took account of the levels of aggregation (as Cor Meijer referred to it) and of specificity; recognising the different needs of individual schools (along the lines of Klaus Wedell). In this continuum of levels it was important to move towards resourcing what is generally available. But he did not see this trend excluded the possibility of some allocation at the individual needs level. Flexible thinking and use of this continuum was needed. In all this, he emphasised that the objectives of inclusion had to be clear, and that if resources were devolved too rapidly there might be a problem of who clears up the mess. However, he also pointed out that delegation had also to take account of the contribution of learning and behaviour support services. Resource allocation schemes had a major impact on their existence and how they worked. The other area which had not been touched on in the resource allocation agenda was the question of SEN specialisation and the deskilling of teachers. In his view there was a place for specialists working in joint collaborative ways. In his experience, some parents have also been contesting the reduction in special school places. The seminar had not addressed the question of the closure of special schools. Some special schools will have to close. His final comment was that we needed a resource allocation system which avoided undesirable strategic behaviour, to use Cor Meijer's phrase.